P9-DZY-265

house beautiful

storage

THE EDITORS OF HOUSE BEAUTIFUL MAGAZINE

LOUIS OLIVER GROPP
Editor in Chief

MARGARET KENNEDY
Editor

Text by
SALLY CLARK

HEARST BOOKS
new york

It is the policy of William Morrow and Company, Inc., and its imprints and affiliates, recognizing the importance of preserving what has been written, to print the books we publish on acid-free paper, and we exert our best efforts to that end.

Clark, Sally.
House beautiful storage / the editors of House beautiful magazine
: Louis Oliver Gropp, editor-in-chief : Margaret Kennedy, editor :
text by Sally Clark.
            p.   cm.
     ISBN 0-688-15098-5
     1. Storage in the home.   2. Interior decoration.   I. House
beautiful.   II. Title.
NK2117.S8H68   1998
747.7'9--dc21
                                           98-14962
                                           CIP

PRINTED IN THE UNITED KINGDOM

First Edition

10   9   8   7   6   5   4   3   2   1

EDITOR
arlene hamilton stewart

ART DIRECTOR
tomek lamprecht

DESIGNERS
carol bokuniewicz design

and paola pelosi

produced by smallwood & stewart, inc., new york

contents

STORAGE IS ABOUT HIDING THINGS, OR SHOWING THEM OFF.

Put another way, you can decide whether you want your storage

open or closed. Of course, you can have both. Most of us do. For

storage is essentially a matter of what you have, where you use it,

and where you want it kept. Any box can hide things, but one that

conceals while beguiling the eye has more flair.

Think point of use. Is this something you use in the dressing

room, the dining room, the bedroom, or

bath? The book to follow is organized in

foreword

just that way, by point of use. But remember that a good idea in a

dining room or kitchen may be just as useful in a bedroom or bath.

Sally Clark's thoughtful, informative text will help you see

beyond the beautiful photographs to the sound storage solutions

developed by many creative designers and homeowners. Adopt the

ideas that suit you with conviction, and we promise that your life

will become not only more visually attractive but more practical

and livable as well.

Louis Oliver Gropp
Editor-in-Chief

STORAGE IS AS MUCH AN ASPECT of design as are color, proportion, and furniture arrangement. Less may be the essence of the modern esthetic, but more appears to be the reality, at least as far as possessions are concerned. We seem to own more clothes, more books, more electronic equipment, more cookware, more china—more of everything—and all of it needs to be stored in a manner that is attractive, yet accessible.

introduction

House Beautiful Storage can help you organize your home. The book is divided into sections: The first offers creative storage ideas for living rooms, family rooms, media rooms, and libraries. The important topic of storage for books is presented with a host of design possibilities, from traditional library cabinetry to modern glass-and-steel-trimmed shelving systems.

Next, storage related to dining is considered. Dining room furniture—sideboards, dressers, dumbwaiters—appears in forms classic and innovative along with built-ins such as cupboards.

Kitchens in both traditional and contemporary styles offer inspiring ideas for a variety of storage components, including cabinet design, shelving, and overhead storage.

Private havens—bedrooms, bathrooms, and dressing rooms—are then presented. Every storage element needed to make these sanctuaries work is considered, from classic furnishings, such as the vanity table and night table, to smart solutions for storing toiletry, linens, and lingerie.

The storage ideas come from homes across the country and different parts of the world. From the English library of the late Nancy Lancaster to the study of a chic Parisian, there are myriad possibilities for storing books. Intriguing combinations of open and closed storage appear in a sleek contemporary California kitchen as well as in a farmhouse-style cookery in New England.

By examining and considering these ideas, you can create your own solutions. In the process you will discover what designers know: When storage is well organized, life falls into place.

living

living storage

STORAGE. THE WORD IS SO FUNCTIONAL AND

the function is so necessary. Yet storage is virtually unmentioned by

many of America's celebrated designers who have taken up the pen

to jot down their thoughts on the art of decoration and room

arrangement. Elsie de Wolfe, Dorothy Draper, and Billy Baldwin all

wrote wonderfully informative books on decorating, sharing their

visions of color, fabrics, and furniture. But not one word did they

utter about storage. When an issue comes down to crafting a built-

in cabinet or buying a piece of freestanding furniture—the two

forms storage usually takes—

perhaps designers found it too

obvious to discuss. For one commission, Baldwin did design a pri-

vate TV/dressing room, lining the room with shelves and hanging

curtains on tracks to draw over them. But the designer did not call

it storage. Today we recognize that it was indeed storage.

A small revolution is occurring in design. Things that

were once hidden, considered mundane and functional aspects of

room planning, are now being embraced as serious aspects of

high-style design. Leading the revolution are some of today's

most famous style-conscious designers, who consider it well

In a whole-house organization plan, ample storage starts at the front hall and appears in every room beyond. In an entrance hall with walls embellished with faux stone decorative painting, designers Lynn Jacobson and Richard Ohrbach cleverly slipped a roomy, well-illuminated hall closet behind a curved book wall. Sliding open at a touch, the tall bookcase holds a small library of favorite volumes.

within their creative scope to organize all of a client's belongings in ways that are both attractive and efficient.

"What is design but the creation of orderliness?" asks Mary Douglas Drysdale. The designer speaks for her peers who, like her, devote much of their professional time to architectural design, reworking spaces and molding fresh interiors. Shaping space is a process that engages a designer in examining storage requirements by room type and devising solutions which have an impact not only on the appearance of the room, but on the pleasure it gives to the people who live there.

Form precedes function in a cupboard designed to keep pace (above) with the whimsical pieces in designer David Livingston's California living room. The cupboard is one of the most versatile storage devices, being comfortable in any room throughout the house. ● In a welcoming gesture, designer Jonathan Straley created a floating semi-wall (opposite) with deep book niches to give the illusion of a cozy book-lined vestibule at the entry to his San Francisco loft.

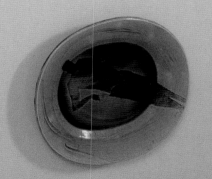

Who would guess this family room (opposite) was once the garage? When the owners of a San Francisco ranch house asked April Sheldon to revamp the 1950s house, she shook up rooms with her unconventional brand of decorating. Her design for a storage wall is atypical, too—a honeycomb of square niches. ● Designer Bunny Williams warms to the coziness of book-filled rooms. In the library (overleaf) of her country house, books crowd the shelves of bookcases and spill onto an ottoman, the circular library table, and every available surface.

Personalization is one of the most important facets of the new interest in storage. We want our storage designed just for us, for the way we live and use our homes. We are more than ever concerned about the most private areas of the house—the bathroom, the bedroom, and the dressing room. New York designer Vicente Wolf is particularly attuned to the shift in focus that has occurred. "In the '80s we were concerned with the public rooms. But in the '90s the attention is on private rooms," says Wolf.

The creativity designers display in devising storage solutions is impressive. William Hodgins, the dean of Boston designers, is a connoisseur of fine antiques and a brilliant space planner. But he is not above training his eye on such details as the design of a night-stand or dressing room commode. Mary Douglas Drysdale avoids the habit of the popular norm. Frustrated by the paltry dimensions of the standard medicine cabinet, for example, she now builds floor-to-ceiling cabinets into all the baths she designs.

The process designers use offers inspiration. Anyone can become fluent in the language of storage. The more creative one becomes with storage solutions the more one recognizes the potential freedom and design impact they can lend to any home.

sophisticated
visibility

A BIT ART DECO, A BIT VIENNA 1900, THIS ROOM delightfully redefines the family den and reinvents its storage, too.

Unique concepts are the stock-in-trade of Manhattan designers Jorge Letelier and Sheryl Asklund Rock. Even so, fashioning a circular plan for a turreted room in one of New York City's grand turn-of-the-century apartment buildings, says Rock, "was quite a challenge. The room is not precisely round; it is slightly, jarringly off." The study was created for a family as a retreat for reading, writing, playing board games, and relaxing. Yet another bookcase-lined study would have been too typical a solution for this project. Letelier and Rock proposed instead something unique: a spare, luminous room as different from a standard study as night is from day. In place of a study's customarily serious and dark palette, the room shimmers with light, its pale tones ranging from white to a café-au-lait tint of beige. Windows are covered not with heavy draperies, but with airy scrims of sun-filtering linen gauze. Most unusual of all in a room dedicated to reading: there are no massive bookshelves.

The designers' brief called for a family den, but bookshelves encroaching on the walls would have interrupted the beautiful curve of this circular space (opposite and overleaf). So New York City designers Jorge Letelier and Sheryl Asklund Rock booked different shelf space—under the seats of the custom-made sofas. They also hollowed out angular niches in side tables attached to the sofas. An ottoman doubling as a cocktail table throws a curve: Its cover is tied on with bungee cord.

A curved, wall-hugging sweep of bookcases concentrates storage low down, at dado height, and terminates in a tower rising parallel to a doorway. Like the rest of the custom-built furniture in this sophisticated family room, the bookcase is made of bleached ashwood and "designed to be wipeable," says Rock. The top of the lowslung bookcase features a surface of sandblasted glass standing on little feet of brushed steel. Another streamlined idea, the televison is installed so that it forms an almost-smooth plane with the wall. Double bands of molding neatly frame the opening.

a structure of storage

WHEN STORAGE IS BUILT INTO THE FABRIC OF
the architecture, it is possible to achieve the most personal
accommodation of one's possessions, as proven by a contemporary
San Francisco apartment. Once a rabbit warren of traditional boxy
rooms, it was completely gutted and meticulously reconfigured
by the firm Turnbull, Griffin, Haesloop as a pied-à-terre for a
suburban couple. Eric Haesloop, a company principal who served
as project architect, sculpted
the interior into a landscape
of curved, angled,
open, and closed
spaces. Within the walls, Haesloop built in closets, cabinets, and
shelves to store everything the couple needed for a pleasurable city
life. To reflect their love of reading, Haesloop designed a bed
surrounded by built-in bookshelves and sheathed a study/
guestroom with a built-in bookwall. Behind the curving walls of
the media room, he concealed a built-in bar and storage for a
large-screen TV. When the couple spoke of sit-down dinners
for twelve, Haesloop took inventory of all the china and dining
implements required and built storage space in both the small

kitchen and into the curved walls of the dining room. Haesloop's working drawings were translated into magnificent custom-built panelled walls and built-in units crafted of honey-colored anegre veneer. To accent the planes of the anegre wood, the architect selected bands of darker cherrywood and inset panels of suede. Both harboring storage and defining space, the woodwork plays across the entire apartment, forming an exquisitely crafted environment that turns shades of gold and honey as sunlight and the recessed lighting wash across it.

Built-in shelves were crafted in the kitchen (left) for glassware and in the combination study and guest room (above) for books. The meticulously built custom storage, designed by project architect Eric Haesloop, was crafted of anegre wood, with cherry and suede accents. Visible in the media room (opposite) are the floors of rippling curly maple and vaulted ceilings with handworked maple slats that run throughout the apartment.

home libraries

FOR THOSE WHO ARE PASSIONATE about books, nothing is like the quiet thrill of being surrounded by them, of having them to see and touch, randomly browse through and reread. People who love books and accumulate them often come to a realization: They do not own their books, the books possess them. For the serious book collector, the arrangement, preservation, and storage of books is an issue worthy of consideration.

What is the best type of bookcase to house a bibliophile's treasure? Built-in bookcases are the ideal storage for those with the space and budget. Built-ins can play up architectural features, setting off a mantelpiece or flanking a doorway. They can completely transform a room, especially when handsome woodwork details are part of the design. Such traditional built-in bookcases are available today from cabinetry firms specializing in custom library installations. Another option is to collaborate

The best way for a book lover to organize a great store of books is to deploy them throughout the house. A bench with gilded arabesques (above) becomes a fetching book table in the Manhattan bedroom of designer Vicente Wolf. ● Striking a much more formal note is the ornate glass-front bookcase (opposite) in the historic Massachusetts home of Henry Wadsworth Longfellow. The great man of letters had half a dozen of these impressive book cabinets nestled against the walls of his equally ornate library.

Like many designers and architects, Robert Dripps and his wife, Lucia Phinney, use their house as a laboratory to test their changing ideas about design. Their two-story library (opposite), built to house their huge book collection, highlights the couple's tendency to find inventive uses for modern materials. On the mezzanine level they installed an unusual glass floor and a see-through "half-wall" of metal crossbars, elements that give the two-story space a luminous airiness. ● In a space-conscious New York City apartment, designer Benjamin Noriega-Ortiz combined lighting and storage requirements in one bold stroke. The phalanx of custom lamps illuminates a wall of books and requires no floor space. ● The grid of the "egg crate" bookcase fills an entire wall of a Manhattan loft (overleaf) and is a signature design of architect Hugh Newell Jacobsen. Beyond its functional role—the bookcase holds 4,000 books—it gives the room a dynamic element.

with a talented independent carpenter who can craft bays set off by simple cornice and base woodwork. Narrow bays are best. "Beyond three feet and the shelves will bow," says Tom Fleming of the New York design firm Irvine & Fleming. "It's a fact of physics."

Of course, to the dedicated bibliophile, the most exciting aspect to building a library is the opportunity to house one's collections in the most protective way. Most volumes need to be kept away from sunlight and extremes in temperature, while many over-sized editions need to be stored vertically with strong support.

at ease with books

THE SPLENDOR OF A LIBRARY, WITH ITS RICH tapestry of leather bindings and colored book spines, is something Nancy Lancaster admired and knew how to work to perfection. After all, the legendary tastemaker's most famous room was a library—the stunning vaulted London interior she called the "Butter Yellow Library," decorated when she was actively involved with Colefax & Fowler, the design firm she bought in 1945. Lancaster treated libraries as sitting rooms rather than sanctums for solitude. As chatelaine of Ditchley Park, a famous English country house designed by the renowned 18th-century Scottish architect James Gibbs, she transformed a pair of faded studies into dazzling libraries. Books, one senses, were one of the elements—along with sun-lit color and soft chairs—that Lancaster used to achieve the lived-in comfort she brought to the English country house interior.

A voracious reader, Lancaster amassed volumes on gardening, decoration, and history, as well as the memoirs of the people she entertained, including Winston Churchill. When she ceased to live in palaces and moved into the comparatively modest quarters of

In the library she created in the orangery, a separate building next to her home, the Coach House, the late Nancy Lancaster had bookcases of the most simple design built to hold her vast collection of books on gardening and decoration. The Virginia-born Lancaster was fond of trompe l'oeil conceits. To disguise the door cut into the book wall, she devised a tableau of glued-on book jackets and paper spines.

The orangery did not have palatial proportions, but Nancy Lancaster gave the modest rooms a grand air with flourishes borrowed from classic stately home decoration. One example: She eliminated the tacked-on look of the bookcases by using the tops of the cabinets to display fine bibelots (left). In the snug blue-and-white sitting room (opposite) small volumes are billeted in the revolving bookcase beside the desk and on the low table in front of it.

her last home, the Coach House, she effortlessly transferred her skill for assembling seductively grand rooms to a smaller venue. Lacking a library, she created one in the orangery, a separate building with a high ceiling and arched windows. She filled the corners and one long wall with bookshelves of the simplest construction: She knew that the tiers of colorful books were decorative enough without embellishing the shelves, too. The arrangement of bookshelves and paintings cascading down walls brought to mind what Cecil Beaton once said about another Lancaster-designed house: "Every nook and corner is of an offhand perfection."

literary legacy

THE TRUE GENIUS OF FRENCH DESIGN IS ITS timelessness, bringing good breeding to any home. In the Paris apartment of Barbara Wirth, symbols of classic French haute style have been reborn in fresh interpretations and arranged with wit by Wirth and Christian Badin, her cousin and partner in a Paris design firm. Winking at the hauteur of the setting, a grand 1790 building in a chic Paris district, they deployed painted wood cypress trees in the foyer and laid crunchy English rush matting on the salon floor. But book collecting is serious business, and for the most suitable storage the pair looked to the French *ébéniste* tradition. The three identical *cartonnier*s Badin had built to hold antiquarian treasures in the salon hint at the magnificence of the cabinetry that lies beyond in the splendid library. There, Badin drew on France's heritage of cabinetwork, a legacy reaching back to the 17th century, but he gave the design a contemporary tweak. The veneered bookcases are set against the walls in continuous banks in the classic French manner, but Badin had them built of cypress instead of the usual oak or walnut. He referred to the French mode of painting a library in contrasting

Parisians developed an appreciation for owning books and a flair for housing them as early as the 17th century. By the 18th century the *cartonnier* had become a venerable furniture form that would stand near a writing table. The updated version created by designer Christian Badin has a top compartment fitted for antique folios and a lower cabinet.

In *The Decoration of Houses*, the influential book on interior design by Edith Wharton and Ogden Codman, published in 1897, the authors write admiringly of the French genius for designing private libraries. "France led the way," they note. "The possession of a library, hitherto the privilege of kings, of wealthy monasteries, came to be regarded as a necessity to every gentleman's establishment." Cultivating that tradition in Wirth's apartment, Badin fitted books everywhere, running shelves above the doorway and into the narrow bay that rises to form a pedestal for an obsidian bust (opposite). The trove of books in her library is so great that volumes overflow into stacks on the floor and steps of the library ladder (above).

As the author of a book on the history of elegant French table settings, Barbara Wirth has a special interest in beautiful dining rooms. Her smartly costumed room (above) requires a slew of china and crystal patterns for the many parties she hosts. To house her precious collection of tableware, Wirth has a towering dining room closet fitted with adjustable shelves (opposite).

colors, too. But he risked the surprise of contemporary colors. Sharp new-leaf green was his choice for the walls, accented with the browns of the faux-bois painted molding strips he applied as embellishment. The dining room is remarkable for its seasonal transformations. The cream colored room is airy in spring and summer, but in the winter, the room is warmed up with red and blue fabric panels slipped into baseboard and cornice channels, and with chairs and tables dressed in a red wool coating fabric. In the blazing room, Badin tinkered with a classic Gallic design: the Louis XVI chair. He reworked its oval back, playfully knocking it sideways in his beechwood version. For the storage of Wirth's huge hoard of china, however, Badin opened the door to the universal language of design. His solution: Two big, roomy closets, as big and deep as he could make them.

"THE RAPPORT BETWEEN WORK AND HOME IS

going to create a new civilization," predicts Charlotte Perriand,

assessing the century as it slips into the next millennium. Perriand

is one of the great pioneers of modern design: As a young woman

in the 1920s and 1930s, she collaborated with Le Corbusier and

Pierre Jeanneret in the creation of tubular metal furniture

work at home

designs—including storage units—that 70 years later stand

as glittering emblems of 20th-century modernism. When this

French visionary makes a pronouncement on contemporary

life, attention must be paid. Perriand is correct, of course: Statistics

on the increasing number of people working at home point

to this phenomenon of incredible—

and global—impact.

Few new houses built today are

without some kind of office space.

Leading designers say that among the

Sarah Spongberg's quiet Massachusetts library is a study in efficient and uncluttered storage. The spare, turn-of-the-century Mennonite table tucked in a windowed corner serves as an inspirational computer station, while floor-to-ceiling bookcases keep texts and stereo equipment close at hand.

Known for clever and colorful designs, Agnes Bourne and Geoffrey DeSousa put a humorous twist on the home office (opposite) in this vanilla room sparked by mango-striped upholstery and chartreuse draperies. A jungle-gym-like bookcase, slipped under a work surface, increases storage potential. Oversized numerals serve as handles on the tall ashwood file cabinets that flank the computer station (left).

most frequently requested renovation projects for existing residences, the home office is just behind kitchens, baths, and master suites. As work comes home, the synthesis of interiors with telecommunications and storage requirements needs to be rethought and reworked to accommodate a new reality.

The most-wanted home office is a separate room dedicated to function and comfort, ideally like the one by Agnes Bourne and Geoffrey DeSousa (the design director of Bourne's San Francisco firm). With creamy pale walls and a radiant mango-colored carpet underfoot, the room has a colorfully upholstered section for group meetings and two ample desk areas. And if its owner glances up for a moment of creative inspiration, breathtaking views of

Designer Anne Marie Vingo opened up a closet, creating two work areas in one space. In the outer room (left), she brought in a Louis XVI–style *bureau plat* as a laptop station and added storage under a window seat. A work area (opposite) shoehorned into the reworked closet abounds with storage—shelves above the desk and recessed-panel file cabinets below. "Custom-made," says Vingo. "You can build in the same idea with custom cabinets and it's not that much more expensive than standard files."

the Golden Gate Bridge and the dark sapphire bay it sweeps over fill the large uncurtained window.

Lacking an extra room, however, one can take inspiration from a section of an interior by Anne Marie Vingo, another San Francisco designer. She carved a hard-working desk and storage area out of a former closet. These two northern California home offices share an important element: Both have plenty of newly discovered storage. Vingo made upper walls functional with shelving, then tucked large lateral file cabinets under the desk in the office. Bourne and DeSousa slid a bookcase and a file cabinet under the work table, then settled a smaller bookcase on top of it.

"I DO NOT WANT AN ELABORATE INSTALLATION to hide my television any more than I want slipcovers for my pianos," said Cole Porter when he hired the legendary Billy Baldwin to design his aerie high in Manhattan's Waldorf Towers. Baldwin agreed. While he was a great advocate of slipcovers for sofas, he loathed coyness in design: Radios, televisions, and telephones, Baldwin believed, needed to be placed out in the open where people use them. Some 60 years later, the TV screen has exploded

storage
for leisure

to wall-size proportions, but the challenge of designing a room with electronics has not changed much at all. It may be a room where family and friends, adults and children, gather to watch the latest video or a newsmaking sports event. Or it may be a more private retreat, dedicated to the solitary enjoyments of listening to music or studying a video to master the art of French cooking. The comfort of the

Tuning in to a comfy idea for bedroom viewing, designers John Stedila and Tim Button set the TV/computer monitor in a high mahogany frame so it can be seen easily from the bed. Then they made a night table to keep a workaholic in bed: The table has an armature poised on a castor. A flick of the wrist and it snuggles up to the bed as a desk for a laptop.

Bringing order to a profusion of electronic equipment, CDs, and cassettes is a design problem that invites ingenious solutions. Designer Eve Robinson's clever idea is the entertainment center built into the wall of the living room of her Manhattan apartment. Interior shelves (opposite) tailored to the size of the equipment are concealed behind sliding stainless steel mesh doors. The shimmer of the doors is reiterated in the silver, bronze, and white satin stripes of the fabric on a contemporary slipper chair (right).

people using the technology is still the most important consideration. The positioning of the TV and stereo, and the storage for CDs, videos, and cassettes, has to be part of a well thought-out plan with an eye to the placement of seating and sources of light. Chairs and sofas should be at a comfortable distance and height and offer various means of support. Cassettes and videotapes should be accorded their own accessible storage spots. Add to that the seductive comfort of the materials, pillows, and colors, and you've created a cocoon of warmth and intimacy. When all design elements are working in concert, enjoying modern technology truly becomes the rewarding leisure activity it was meant to be.

At the center of a perfectly square room (right), Washington, D.C. designer José Solis placed a square coffee table of his own design. It doubles as a concealing cabinet for stereo equipment and a projection TV (above). The screen is mounted opposite a pair of cushiony armchairs and near a daybed with piles of downy soft pillows. ● In the living room (overleaf) of an actress, designer DD Allen carved out custom-sized niches for TV, stereo, and videotapes. To camouflage the storage and link the area to the room's plush traditional decor, the designer hung a tapestry to slide in front of the screen.

keepers and niches

ANY CONTAINER OR NICHE CAN HIDE THINGS, but the one that conceals while beguiling the eye has flair. Sometimes, the most charming niche or keeper is one that starts out life as something else. A niche can be found space, tucked under a stair or above a beam—to name but two. The cache can take the form of a box, a basket, a wall pocket, an urn, or a sentimental favorite old hat. The shape, color, finish, and workmanship are some of the qualities that will set a desirable object apart. The object may be simple or ornate. It can be an antique of fine pedigree. Or it can be a serendipitous discovery. A writer who treasure-hunts at country estate sales and church bazaars has filled her house with unique furnishings bought for a song. Her favorite keeper is a small gold-foil-covered creation of paperboard shaped like a king's crown in which, appropriately for a writer, she keeps stamps and paper clips.

Some of the most gratifying stowaway places are niches and odd hiding holes concealed in the architectural fabric of a room. The abundance of found-storage hideaways in old houses is one reason some people are enamored of antique dwellings. There is

The man readers knew as Mark Twain was no doubt impressed by the study Louis Comfort Tiffany designed for him in his Hartford, Connecticut, home. But when he got down to work, he escaped to the organized clutter in his billiard room (above). ● When Atlanta designer Dan Carithers first laid eyes on a spanking new builder house, he missed the presence of decorative woodwork, so he filled out a recess (opposite) with niches, shell cap, and curving shelves.

Precious under-the-stairs storage space might have gone to waste, but architects Susan Lanier and Paul Lubowicki added two small raised-panel doors and turned the area into a hideaway that might be used for luggage or seasonal items (opposite). ● In a guest room of Patricia Trainor's farmhouse, the area above a bedroom window (right) provides a perch for a board with over-sized pegs. A line-up of hats waits to go on country walks.

something so enchanting about discovering a cabinet under an old stairway or an oddly shaped niche hidden behind a 200-year-old panelled door. Many older homes contain large closets or small rooms built in unexpected places, which can be annexed into rooms or outfitted with shelves to hold books and collections. Airing rooms, boxing rooms, sewing rooms, butler's pantries, and small porches are often left alone, their storage potential unmined. Other older homes might feature wide stairway landings with built-in benches and window seats with tops that open to reveal an ample storage space.

Pockets of storage can be created even in freshly minted rooms. An oddly shaped niche might be cut into the space under a stairway, or a shallow cupboard might be scooped out of a corridor wall and shuttered with salvaged doors. Undersized medicine and linen closets can often be expanded by opening up the spaces in between wallboard studs and adding wider shelving. The newly made niche might be a crisply modern affair, say a cubbyhole built into a wall in a bedroom and lined with exotic wood or even steel. Such a detail offers much more than a whimsical hiding place: It chases anonymity from a too-brand-new space and bestows upon it a measure of human warmth.

Who can guess what items might be concealed behind the doors of the salvaged mantel (opposite) that designers Charles Spada and Tom Vanderbeck installed in their Connecticut country house? ● Finders need keepers. Some people like to stash things they collect in boxes. Others, like designer Thomas O'Brien, are passionate for baskets. He filled the rooms of his country house with every shape and type of reedy vessel. In this woven keeper (right), he shelters his camera and keepsake snapshots.

dining

BY THEIR SHEER QUANTITY AND VARIETY, THE accoutrements of elegant dining hold a top position in the roll call of household objects. Most items associated with dining involve multiples—multiple sets of china (for breakfast, luncheon, buffet) and multiple sets and types of glasses (stemware, barware, casual, and formal) that form a wardrobe of styles for different occasions and meals. Not to mention the pitchers, tureens, platters, and condiment pieces that play a role in the presentation of a meal.

elements for dining

Flatware and linens add even more objects to the dining inventory. Storing this abundance of china, glassware, and silver raises an intriguing question: kitchen or dining room? Certainly it is reasonable to house everything associated with meals in the kitchen. But there is something very appealing about having at least some accessories in the dining room. Designer Gretchen Mann has discovered what many accomplished hosts come to realize: How convenient it is to have the elements of dining organized and displayed in the room where they are most often used and enjoyed.

Capitalizing on the beauty of the cream-painted Federal corner cupboard in her New England dining room, designer Gretchen Mann filled the shelves with white ironstone serving pieces and then loaded more of them on a buffet ledge. For meals and parties, the serving pieces are there to both use and admire.

Looking much as it did in the 1700s, the original portion of designer Laura Bohn's country house (opposite) is graced with many colonial-era storage devices: built-in cupboards, shelves, even a hidden staircase behind the fireplace on which to dry muddy boots. ● Tricia Foley is not at all fazed by the lack of closets in her Victorian weekend cottage. As a professional stylist and author of design books, she is accustomed to challenges. Her resourceful solution for the closetless dining room is a rustic pine cupboard (right) with broad interior shelves to hold chinaware, serving pieces, and part of her collection of vintage linens.

"Dining rooms are rooms we really need to study and think about in terms of storage," says Washington, D.C., designer Mary Douglas Drysdale. "If you love china, if you entertain often, you need to find a convenient place to store everything." Drysdale likes concealed storage in dining rooms and has worked out many ingenious designs for it. When a client has a formal dining room, Drysdale often embellishes the room with large urns. To support the urns she creates sturdy five-foot-high pedestals, which offer a surprising storage bonus. "I always design storage space in the

A cream-painted butler's cart performs the pampering functions of a wait staff in a dining room by designer Bunny Williams (opposite). A connoisseur of furniture who began her career in a fine antiques shop, Williams often likes to solve storage problems with an interesting piece of furniture. ● The late architectural designer Benjamin Baldwin preferred clean-lined built-ins. "To me, furniture is the least important part of an interior, and I always feel the less of it, the better," Baldwin once stated. Cleaving to his principle, he set a bank of low cabinets against the wall in a client's dining room (right) and built an additional complex of vertical cabinets a few feet away. The cabinetry fades into the off-white wall, allowing one to focus on the artwork and plants congregating on the cabinet.

pedestals' interiors so people can put their crystal or china in them," says Drysdale. She also conceals storage for china and glassware behind tall panelled walls that her master cabinetmaker crafts for a formal dining room. "It looks like Georgian panelling, but it is actually a series of blind doors operated by touch latches," says Drysdale of one such installation she completed for party-giving clients who needed a large storage area for umpteen sets of china.

Touch-latch cabinetry unobtrusively masks storage areas and can be built to suit either traditional or modern styles of decoration. The design may be spare and simple, consisting of flat-panel doors painted the same color as the room so that the storage area blends with the walls. Or it can be more elaborate cabinetry with 18th- or 19th-century period detailing made out of fine wood. Whatever style, built-ins are not only an asset to storage capacity, they're an asset to the value and beauty of a room. Anyone fortunate enough to own an antique house with an authentic period corner cupboard, a breakfront, or a well-outfitted butler's pantry knows how convenient it is to have this timeless storage already in place, still beautiful, still efficient.

Design team Paul Mathieu and Michael Ray relaxed an apartment in France by installing an entire wall of cabinetry in the dining room and kitchen (opposite). A pass-through, a convention pulled from generations past, is concealed behind a short curtain. ● In an 18th-century farmhouse in France's Provençal countryside, every element of the dining room (left) adds to the serenity. The old china cabinet shares peeled-paint simplicity with an endearing battered plank table and caned-backed Louis XVI chairs.

RESIDENCES BECOME ALL THE MORE welcoming when there are visible signs of entertaining, and lack of space is no excuse. The drinks tray, which the English manage to squeeze into the tiniest quarters, is an emblem of hospitality urbane Americans have taken up with enthusiasm. A butler's tray on sturdy legs provides ample space for half a dozen bottles, yet takes up only a few feet of space. A Victorian mahogany cabinet or a small

planned to entertain

American country cupboard would also work nicely. Accoutrements found at estate sales add panache: a hotel silverplated ice bucket and tongs, cocktail napkins from the 1950s with amusing appliqués, heavy cut-crystal whiskey glasses and small crystal bowls, and nests of trays.

In the cozy hall of his Manhattan Belle Epoque apartment (above), decorator Richard Keith Langham welcomes guests with a jigger of his Southern hospitality. A hall table, crowned by a bookcase, displays a well-stocked drinks tray. ● Designer Barbara Barry toasted the classic English drinks table by designing her own model (opposite) with sinuously curved legs and setting it in an alcove with shelves full of stacked boxes.

As every host knows, the effortless-looking cocktail celebration or dinner party rests on a foundation of sound planning. Storage organization is vital to the successful event. Part of that planning includes having a well-organized arsenal of supplies: closets and

Serving at parties is a snap for Carol Glasser, who chooses her presentation pieces from the impressive collection of Staffordshire platters, tureens, and over-sized bowls openly displayed on the shelves of her colossal English pine dresser (opposite). "I just take them down and use them," says the Houston designer. • Concealed storage is Marjorie Reed Gordon's preference. The dining room walls of her New York City apartment are lined with beautifully designed built-in cabinets painted and wood-trimmed like fine old European armoires (left). Inside are drawers for linens and adjustable shelves to accommodate the platters and glasses in Gordon's immense collection of party crystal and accessories.

cupboards with shelves so well-arranged that it is easy to find and retrieve china, glassware, and serving pieces. One's storage selection may be an antique dresser with shelves for open display and a cupboard below. A more contemporary style, such as modern built-in cabinets or a freestanding piece, are alternatives. Whatever its design, the carefully thought-out storage plan for party tableware and accessories will make for an event that is truly entertaining—for the hosts as well as the guests.

One of the pioneers of modernism, Marcel Breuer carried his philosophy of pared-down functional design from the Bauhaus straight to the houses he designed in post-war America of the 1940s and 1950s. A signature of a Breuer house is built-in cabinetwork, a direct reflection of his youthful role as head of the Bauhaus's joinery and cabinetry workshop. Desks, cabinets, bookshelves, and credenzas were conceived as part of the interior architecture, a design tactic that produced spacious interiors even when rooms were small. In a Baltimore house Breuer designed in 1959, recently restored by New York architect Jonathan S. Foster, the built-in marble-topped credenza in the dining room shows Breuer's sympathy for natural wood and stone materials. It is all the storage this room needs for the host to entertain in a grand style.

Designer Bill Blass's Connecticut country
house was originally a tavern, and that
tradition of hospitality is kept alive by the
convivial fashion designer. When he
entertains on weekends, candlesticks,
decanters and carafes are all sparkling and
ready for use in a cupboard (above). ●
For a dedicated oenophile who entertains
frequently, having storage capacity for
many cases of wine is an important
consideration. Magnificent storage walls of
the wine cellar (right) were constructed with
deep bays large and sturdy enough to hold
numerous bottles from a single vineyard or
vintage. The custom-crafted ladder makes
upper bays accessible.

THE ORNAMENTAL BEAUTY OF THE elements of dining invites them to be displayed and admired. Historically, open display in the dining room was born from reasons reaching beyond the practical need for storage. In the 18th century, when the idea of a separate room for dining emerged, the contents of the dining room's built-in cupboards served as a

furniture that stores

discreet advertisement of a family's wealth and status displaying china and silver for all to admire. Today, open display is used for purposes decorative and functional, rich in the show of color, pattern, shapes, and surfaces.

Dressers are one of the oldest forms of furniture associated with dining and display, borrowing their name directly from the pine board on which food was "dressed," or prepared before serving. Once the mainstay of every kitchen, plebeian and patrician, the often immense country dresser can hold a trove of pottery,

Shaking antique walls awake, furniture designers Monique and Sergio Savarese wheeled a stainless steel cabinet into the dining area of their Pennsylvania farmhouse (opposite). ● Completely in period is the 18th-century form of the Connecticut corner cupboard with its bluish-green paint (above) in the dining room of the New England farmhouse of designers Peter Ermacora and Evan G. Hughes.

The overscale size of a late-Georgian cabinet (above) lends a sumptuous air to the small sitting-dining room of London designer Charles Beresford-Clark. Originally an upstairs-landing cupboard, the piece's beveled-glass–fronted cabinets and numerous drawers in graduating sizes offer a marvelous union of protected display storage and concealed storage. ● An American country chest and armoire (opposite), customarily used for clothing in a bedroom, successfully masquerades as a linen press in a garden dining room. ● Designer John Saladino chose an elaborate Continental cabinet for a Connecticut fieldstone house (overleaf).

plates, and kitchenware on open and closed shelves.

Much more formal are the elegant breakfront and sideboard. The breakfront made its debut in the 17th century when Europeans began collecting costly Oriental china and needed a place to store their expensive wares. One hundred years later, the sideboard became a fixture in the dining rooms of the newly wealthy merchant class. With its deep drawers for linens, slit drawers for flatware, and a generous surface to hold fine sterling silver candelabra and a tea or coffee service, the sideboard is a highly versatile piece of furniture—and timeless. It has been interpreted by cabinetmakers working in styles ranging from 18th-century Georgian to 20th-century Art Deco.

Butler's carts and dumbwaiters are two other storage stalwarts. Multiple tiered surfaces make the dumbwaiter an ideal silent servant for holding condiments and bunches of flatware, while plates or glasses can be organized conveniently on the shelves of a butler's cart on duty near the table. The Canterbury, another

faithful dining room servant, has been moonlighting in other jobs for years: Invented in the 18th century as a supper trolley to hold plates and forks beside the table, it became a music rack in the 19th century and a magazine and newspaper caddy in the 20th. Rolling back into the dining room now, the Canterbury makes a wonderful storing place for trays and platters, or even a handy spot for the family's napkins and napkin rings.

Although Washington, D.C., designer Mary Douglas Drysdale hates clutter, she could not hide the shimmering light of a stellar example of silversmithing. She set a fine tea set and its exquisite gallery tray on a Sheraton sideboard (opposite), where its silvery radiance reflects on the polished mahogany surface. ● In a new Hudson River Valley home designed by architect Heather Faulding, the deep shelves of a rustic cabinet (left) provide storage for linens, china, and spirits.

kitchens

kitchen rethought

IN THE WELL-FURNISHED KITCHEN, STORAGE is everything. The matte-black granite counter, the steel-clad professional range—these may be objects we desire in the kitchen of our dreams, but the real luxury we covet is storage, and plenty of it. We also want storage that can be dedicated to very specific culinary purposes: shelves to hold cans and food packages, drawers with dividers to impose order on utensils, regimented slots to hold trays and platters at attention. Each of us carries our own personal list of storage must-haves, formulated according to the way we cook and entertain and the complexity of the menus we create.

At designer Christian Liaigre's island house off the coast of France, guests need no help finding their way around the kitchen: The host thoughtfully built open shelves to stack tableware in view. And what is the unkitcheny black cabinet finish? Tar stain, Liaigre tells visitors, amused that his cupboards share the same stain with which local sailors waterproof their boat hulls. In storage design, the best solutions are often creative expresssions of individual style.

As a suitable complement to the simplicity of his 18th-century weekend house on the Île de Ré, French designer Christian Liaigre had the kitchen's cabinets and open shelves constructed in a bold and simple style. The counter and upright supports are water-impervious teak. A stack of aluminum canisters adds to the monochromatic elegance.

"POINT OF USE!" THAT IS THE NEW rallying cry of kitchen designers about the placement of storage in a well-planned kitchen. Knives near the chopping board, pots near the cooktop. When storage areas cluster around the kitchen's work centers, step-saving efficiency is assured.

"Zoning" is the operative command in intelligent

open and closed

kitchen design. All well-thought-out kitchens have zones of activity—the preparation zone, the cooking zone, the serving zone, and the clean-up zone. Recognizing and maximizing the potential organization of each activity zone heightens the pleasure of working and spending time in the kitchen.

As kitchens explode in size, zoning is increasingly important because it breaks the room into manageable hubs of productivity. The most spacious kitchens frequently boast at least two cooking zones, several preparation zones, and more than one clean-up area.

A master at manipulating the subtle power of white, designer Vicente Wolf used the wide edges of a trio of open shelves to build drama in a pristine white kitchen (opposite). He echoed the shape of the shelves in the soffit construction, creating a gallery for vintage cookie jars. ● In a Boston kitchen, the 1915 butler's pantry cabinet (above) was so charming that designers Arrel Linderman and Sudie Schenck preserved it to hold a collection of majolica. The tiered rack shelters pots.

Designer Lou Ann Bauer concocted a zesty mix of storage options for clients who wanted furnishings that look assembled—not built in—for their renovated turn-of-the-century San Francisco kitchen. Bauer's recipe called for a mixture of under-counter cabinets for closed storage and above-counter cherry and pine fixtures. Above the sink (opposite), an old-fashioned open dish rack holds plates and cups. Below the cherrywood counter (left), are open basket drawers brimming with produce; above it, a ledge of crown molding summons a line-up of glass storage jars.

Each hub needs its own storage plan. The best way to orchestrate storage is to develop a comprehensive punch list detailing the equipment, utensils, and minor and major appliances required to make each center of activity flow smoothly.

Open or closed? This decision depends on personal habits and esthetics. In an open-storage plan, shelves shoulder the burden of organization and appearances. For that reason, open shelves require careful attention. Details count: An extra-wide lip on the shelves or an imaginative storage grid will impose a sharp edge on the wall and that will, in turn, influence the style of the entire kitchen.

A pull-out storage cupboard (opposite), designed by Cecilia Campa, provides a San Francisco kitchen with storage that appears and disappears as needed. ● To capitalize on every inch of space in fashion designer Han Feng's tiny Manhattan kitchen (right), architect Scott K. James hung a double track of above-counter cabinets. A rolling ladder zooms around the kitchen on a metal track, making it possible to reach cabinets and shelves. ● As a counterpoint to the stainless steel in a California kitchen (overleaf), designer John Saladino eased in an antique French cabinet.

Of course, the greatest advantage of closed storage over open storage is that it always makes a kitchen look as neat as a pin. When cabinet doors close, clutter disappears. Open storage requires extra maintenance to keep it organized looking and not distracting. Bear in mind, though, that when designing large areas of closed storage, cabinetry becomes a forceful element, dictating color, texture, and the character of the room. The risk in having a panorama of cabinetry is that the kitchen may feel suffocatingly "boxy," especially if the cabinets are solid wood or dark finishes.

by the architect

METAL. WOOD. CONCRETE. FROM THESE RAW, modest materials, Fu-Tung Cheng expertly crafts kitchens that become works of art. In one of his kitchens, the unexpected will happen; Countertops of poured concrete glisten with jewellike flecks of turquoise and fossil shells. Light glints off the metal bands smoothly wrapped around counter edges. Cheng designs a kitchen like a champion chess player, carefully deliberating his moves far in advance. His game pieces are materials, space, and light, which he masterfully plays against each other to achieve a near monolithic effect.

Serenity reigns in the typical Cheng-designed kitchen. No clutter intrudes. The voids between the objects are almost more important than the objects themselves. There is a generous amount of storage, most of it concealed behind golden expanses of fir cabinetry crafted to a smooth lustre. Cheng works the wood grain for its beauty, sometimes setting shimmering bands at angles, other times running the satiny ripples in horizontal rows. In this master's hands, cabinets are an evocative device, capable of bestowing on a busy kitchen a peacefulness and tranquility of Zen-like power.

Lurking behind the apparent calmness of this kitchen designed by Fu-Tung Cheng is a subtle tension derived from the designer's careful placement of elements. The zig-zag of bent steel slicing down the wall, for example, is a wine rack—and also a lively angular shape that jolts awake the quiet horizontal elements around it. Metal squares angled into the corners of cabinets are another inventive idea: They are candleholders turned into hardware.

No disorder interrupts the serene quietude
of this kitchen: Utensils, pots, and all
manner of gear are hidden away behind
the fir wood cabinets crafted to show off
lustrous horizontal bands of grain (left). The
minimal glass shelves above the counter
display Asian craft pieces. An opening
beneath the counter is intended for generic
storage—and is large enough to hold
dozens of bottles of spring water or a
woven rattan waste basket. Designer Fu-
Tung Cheng constructed a door in the
island (above) to swing open at the corner,
revealing shelves for large serving pieces.

kitchen
air rights

LOOK UP. MOST PEOPLE FORGET TO.
Overhead space is one of the most promising areas
for storage in a kitchen—yet, sadly, the most frequently under-utilized. Even professional designers
are sometimes guilty of overlooking the pockets of
space above the cabinets. Or, if it is taken into
account, that high-up area is frequently relegated
to a bric-a-brac display rather than active, often-
used storage. Dead space this is
not, but rather, potential air rights
begging to be claimed. A pot rack suspended above a stove may
hold aloft a cook's trove of omelette pans, sauce pots, woks, and
steamers. A shelf raised above a window can cradle wine racks,
cookbooks, and instructional videotapes. Cabinetry that stops a
few inches—or, worse, a few feet—below the ceiling squanders
potentially valuable storage space. A more productive installation is
to construct the cabinets right up to the ceiling line, a maneuver
that can add yards of aerial storage to a good-sized kitchen.

Hovering over the curved laminate island, a
stainless fixture supports an airborne
batterie de cuisine in a kitchen (opposite)
designed by Charles Morris Mount. The
mish-mash of cookware flies in contrast to
the slick sweep of all-concealing cabinets.
● In another feat of aerial storage,
designer Fu-Tung Cheng hoisted a
bracketed shelf high above a window
(above) to warehouse a cook's library of
books and gourmet videotapes.

for the cook

SURROUNDED BY SHELVES BRIMMING WITH A collection of toasty gold Vallauris faïence from Provence and blue-and-white transferware, Jane Ellis is in her element in the renovated kitchen of her Connecticut country home. An accomplished cook and hostess (and *House Beautiful's* food editor), she had longed for the "live-in" kitchens of her English childhood. The opportunity to realize her dream appeared when she and her husband, New York architect William Ellis, bought an 18th-century farmhouse with a kitchen in need of renovation. The cramped little 1950s kitchen had one advantage, an adjacent room that could be incorporated into a larger plan. With the walls reconfigured, William created a flowing farmhouse-style complex with a layout that allows Jane to tend simmering pots and still talk with guests enjoying before-dinner drinks and appetizers around the pine dining table.

In place of wall cabinets, the architect mounted an entire wall of simple open shelves in the cookery area. To set off the wood-work, he painted shelves and brackets white and chose a contrasting bright yellow for the back wall. The sunshine color snaps the room together, even though William describes it as "really a

Farmhouse-style open storage creates a cozy environment in Jane and William Ellis's weekend-house kitchen. Having designed kitchens for such professionals as George Lang and Craig Claiborne, William knew what worked in a kitchen. He planned open shelves around the main work area and stove, and installed shelves in a tall cupboard and adjoining pantry.

washed-out ochre." The distinctive pattern of open and closed storage has an expansive effect on the kitchen, making it feel friendly and seem larger looking, while it affords the maximum efficiency that is so often inherent in this type of arrangement. A sure indication of the redesign's soundness: the Ellises have no desire to redo any of the kitchen. Now, with the implements of her craft all around her and surrounded by comfortable farmhouse furniture and a beloved cast-iron stove, Jane Ellis happily spends weekends cooking and entertaining.

Tucked in a corner of the dining area (opposite), an old English dairy table is decorative and functional storage furniture. Huge salt-glaze crocks tucked on a shelf under the table hold pasta and grains. A worn pine dairy table with drawers cradles an inherited collection of Sheffield knives, sterling forks, dessert spoons, and Victorian serving pieces (right).

KEEPING A KOSHER KITCHEN IS A MATTER OF faith—but it is also a storage challenge. Kosher cooking ordains two sets of pots, utensils, and dishes. That is because orthodox dietary laws forbid mixing meat and dairy or commingling the cookware, china, and utensils used for preparing and serving kosher meals. Designer Joan DesCombes solved the double storage dilemma with a brilliant plan. The Florida designer refashioned the kitchen with two mirror-image areas. On one side of the kitchen, cabinets were constructed to hold pots, plates, and silverware for dairy preparation. Across the room, a twin storage layout holds items used for meals that involve meat. Both pantries are identical; each contains roll-out storage trays, deep adjustable shelves, and slotted vertical sections for large serving trays.

The camel-toned cabinets facing off on both sides of a Florida kitchen (opposite) are part of a storage plan devised by Joan DesCombes for clients who keep a kosher kitchen. Pots, dishes, and utensils for dairy meals are housed in one set of cabinets (above left); those for meat meals are organized in identical shelves and cabinets directly across the room (above right). A sink with three basins keeps the two sets of dishes and cookware further separated.

for the collector

WHITE-PAINTED CABINETRY HAS A MAGICAL

way of appearing airy and luminous. A total white-out was exactly

what a Hollywood producer wanted for the old-fashioned kitchen

she envisioned. Although she had never designed a kitchen before,

the homeowner knew exactly the effect she wanted and how

to achieve it. She cast an array of cabinets in her production,

positioning cupboards with glass doors—some transparent, some

opaque—on upper walls and setting solid wood cupboards with

raised panel doors against lower walls. Behind the triple sink,

casement windows

form a bay that

holds an assemblage of the homeowner's favorite green crockery.

The homeowner made sure to include an abundance of

drawers, too—nearly two dozen of them slide out from beneath the

gray-veined white Carrera marble counters. The quantity of storage

units is not oppressive, and the different styles harmonize, because

all the white-painted surfaces blend and melt away into the walls.

Finally, she positioned her vast collection of crockery pieces:

dozens and dozens of vintage plates, cups, saucers, bowls, jugs—all

in vibrant green colors. She stacked plates on open shelves,

Because the owner likes to live with her collections, the window ledge behind the sink in this all-white kitchen was designed to be deep enough to accommodate a convention of leaf-green, vintage 1930s and 1940s crockery pieces. The kitchenware, with diverse tapered and bulbous silhouettes, lends a spring-like zing to the sunny California room.

suspended cups on hooks under cabinets, crowded vases and jars at counter corners. The glass and crockery are not set pieces; they have been placed out in the open to be used and enjoyed every day. Storage didn't stop with cabinets and shelves. High around the perimeter of the room, baskets and jugs rest on cabinet tops in an airy arrangement. With its charmingly varied white cabinetry and whimsical greenware displays, this kitchen seamlessly combines storage practicality with prettiness, and always gets rave reviews from the hostess's guests.

An amazing variety of green crockery and glass peeks out from open shelves and glass-front cabinets in an all-white kitchen (opposite). Storage features packed into the island include four narrow drawers on metal runners (above) to hold table linens, and niches designed for large pieces of pottery in the owner's favorite color. Drawers at the built-in desk—and throughout the room—sparkle with old glass knobs. Cup hooks stud the interiors and undersides of upper cabinets (right), allowing cups and mugs to be displayed.

by the partners

IN THE RENOVATION OF AN OLDER

kitchen, the question often arises: Should one attempt

to preserve the charm of vintage cabinets or strike out

in a completely new direction? For the husband

and wife architectural team of Taal Safdie and Ricardo

Rabines, there was no debate. A clean-lined,

thoroughly modern design was the most fitting

solution for this townhouse. In the process, the architects replaced

a turn-of-the-century maze of little rooms with a spacious

contemporary

kitchen and dining

area resplendant with a bounty of clever storage ideas.

Custom-made cabinetry sheathes the walls. Made of avodire

wood, a light-colored hardwood from West Africa, the cabinets

are designed so that the exotic tiger grain shimmers in the light that

pours through the large kitchen windows. Cut in square and

rectangular shapes, the cabinets not only lend a look of sleek,

geometry to the space, but provide a variety of storage options.

In the cooking area, open niches punctuate the sleek wood

cabinets, establishing a rhythm of open and closed spaces. Painted

Into the shell of a turn-of-the-century townhouse, architects Taal Safdie and Ricardo Rabines dropped a contemporary kitchen and large storage unit. They created two hallways by building the storage unit in the middle of an open space. One hallway (above) is a study in woodcraft opposites—three-dimensional vintage balusters on the stairs, and flat-panel cabinets on the right. Two buffet tables in the other corridor drop down from hiding places.

In the main work area (left), open niches filled with Oriental artifacts act as visual pauses to the sheaths of elegantly crafted wood cabinet doors. All cookware and utensils are hidden away in this kitchen, but wine is in full view (opposite), slotted into an attractive gridlike holder built especially for bottles. Making the most of overhead storage, deep shelves are shadow boxes for collectibles.

vivid coral red, the niches serve as colorful galleries to display dark lacquer and metal Japanese artifacts. In the breakfast area, additional coral-painted niches continue a progression across the ceiling from the kitchen. Like decorative shadow boxes, each exhibits one or two carefully placed Oriental craft pieces.

Hidden storage in the kitchen and the corridor leading to it is a tribute to the artistry of both the architects and their cabinetmaker: Buffet tables drop down from walls, ingeniously creating additional surface areas so often needed when a large group of friends gathers. When stored upright, the drop-down tables mesh seamlessly, gliding silently like those in a piece of fine furniture.

dressing

well-dressed room

IN THE BYGONE ERA OF LADIES' MAIDS AND gentlemen's valets, the dressing room was a staple feature of a stylishly run house. Conveniently connected to the master bedroom, this separate space offered roomy closets to suit all manner of clothing, from everyday attire and evening gowns to out-of-season apparel that might require a cedar-lined wardrobe. Built-in shelves for hatboxes, handbags, gloves, and shoes, and in larger spaces, sometimes a cheval mirror, a chaise, and a vanity table, were standard appointments of the well-furnished dressing room.

Now that bigger houses seem to be coaxing back some of the cosseting comforts of life, the dressing room is on the return. It is wonderful to have a private place to dress while another sleeps undisturbed—not to mention the convenience of having an organized wardrobe at one's command. But it is possible to enjoy the pleasures of a dressing room even without a separate space. With well-planned storage, a slice of the bedroom or a corner of a walk-in closet can be transformed into a personal haven for

To enhance the manor-house warmth of a dressing and bath area, designer David Anthony Easton enlisted for his storage agenda traditional pieces of furniture equipped with drawers and shelves. The lower shelves of two tables act as open linen closets, holding stacks of fluffy towels. The chest of drawers seen through the doorway stores a wardrobe of gentlemen's sweaters and shirts.

dressing. Permanent shelves and drawers contribute a custom-tailored appearance to such a space. A striking-looking piece of furniture placed in a corner of a room also works well, designating the space around it as an area reserved for dressing and grooming.

Fortunate are those who have the space for a separate dressing room—they can stock it with every type of storage indulgence. In the completely outfitted dressing room, all contingencies would be anticipated. Shelves for luggage would be included, as well as a flat surface for packing. A built-in ironing board along with a storage area for an iron, sewing box, and other paraphernalia dedicated to

The built-in units in the dressing room/ walk-in closet (opposite) of Boston designer William Hodgins's bedroom suite are marvels of precision planning. Utilizing every inch, Hodgins designed a full-height unit with adjustable shelves to accommodate folded sweaters and pairs of shoes. Double-hung metal rods keep suits and shirts smartly crisp. A demi-lune commode off the bedroom (right), also built to his design, offers an abundance of wardrobe storage—even the curved baseboard slides out to serve as a drawer.

the care of a wardrobe would also be provided. Electrical outlets would be near eye-level in mirrored grooming areas where niches and shelves hold hair dryers and other small appliances. Deep shelves and drawers would organize the toiletries we accumulate. In the best suites, a laundry would be tucked inside cabinetry, making it possible to have one's favorite things clean and fresh at hand.

In a dressing room dedicated to a man of style (opposite), Paris designer Yves Germain Taralon slipped a 19th-century neo-classical commode with gilded details into an alcove to serve as a haberdashery cabinet. Interior shelves hold shirts while scarves and belts are nonchalantly draped over the glass doors. On the marble top, crowded with bottles of colognes and sterling toiletry containers, a female bust doubles as a witty hat stand. ● Dee Thornton created a luxurious closet using checked cotton taffeta (left). She lined the walls, then stitched a fold-down "door." Although the closet opening is narrow, shelves are deep enough to store a cache of toiletries, towels, and linens.

A cul-de-sac off a master bedroom (opposite) became an elegant dressing area with the addition of a good-size three-drawer mahogany chest. Manhattan designer Mariette Himes Gomez amplified the small space with the reflective power of large-scale mirrors. ● The bare wood floors of an open-plan dressing room (above) underscore the tactile beauty of the custom cherrywood cabinets commissioned by architects Lee Mindel and Peter Shelton. The freestanding unit opens on all four sides and boasts a dressing table. Facing the unit is a wardrobe wall with floor-to-ceiling hanging storage plus additional drawer space.

shaker
de luxe

In the dressing room (opposite and overleaf) designed by John Saladino, the furniture and storage walls by cabinetmaker Ian Ingersoll are authentically Shaker—down to the lathe-turned knobs. In the absence of clutter, the room becomes pristine. "The Shakers almost never had open shelves," says Ingersoll. They concealed shelves and their contents behind closed doors, "so the room was always neat and tidy."

DRAWING INSPIRATION FROM THE EXQUISITELY handcrafted complexes of drawers and cupboards that Shaker cabinetmakers built along entire walls and around rooms, John Saladino designed a dressing room for the master suite of a Long Island waterfront weekend house. He awarded the cabinetry commission to Ian Ingersoll, a Connecticut master cabinetmaker whose work is acclaimed throughout the design community. Working in rich cherrywood, Ingersoll's studio built two floor-to-ceiling cabinets that flank the entrance to the master bathroom and feature a wealth of storage—groups of short and long drawers, and raised-panel cupboards that open to reveal rows of shelves. Cherrywood blanket chests on each side of the room, used as bureaus, are Ingersoll's finely crafted reproductions of pieces at the Shaker Pleasant Hill Community in Kentucky. A spare trestle table, also cherrywood, with unusually graceful wrought-iron braces, stars at the center of the room as a piece of luxurious functionalism for laying out clothes and packing for travel. Ingersoll's studio also crafted the towering raised-panel doors that open into the bathroom; when they are closed, the doors form a single plane with the storage wall.

baths

the bath

THE RITUAL OF GROOMING CAN BE A HASTY splash of water at the vanity or a slow, indulgent soak in the tub. But whatever the pace of one's daily toilette, having convenient, well-organized storage in the bathroom will make it a pleasure.

To create a bathroom that's as functional, yet as pampering, as possible, storage should cater to the habits and inclinations of the people who use it. Women who prefer to keep their cosmetics in the bathroom, rather than the bedroom, may want extra rows of shelves for containers and jars; men who shave in the shower might appreciate having a built-in accommodation for shaving equipment set at shoulder height in the shower wall. Individual storage can be highly personal: One homeowner insisted on space for a small refrigerator, which kept bottles of cologne icy for her to splash on after stepping from a bracing hot whirlpool bath.

Small appliances make their demands on storage space as well. Who could deny how welcome a shelf would be just for the hair dryer and the army of brushes and combs it seems to attract? A bathroom should have both open and concealed storage to allow for a plethora of soaps, hair care products, bath oils, and pharmacy items. Some toiletries are packaged in beautiful jars and

In a sleek, glamorous bathroom, a witty tiered stand made of wooden thread spools keeps the atmosphere from turning serious. Besides providing generous space, the shelves have curving fronts, which make the hodge-podge of items stored there appear more interesting.

Nothing is worse than stepping from a hot, invigorating shower, reaching for a towel, and discovering—nothing. That never occurs in the bathroom designed by Joan Halperin (opposite), which features a sauna-style mahogany bench with storage beneath for armfuls of fluffy bath sheets. More towels are rolled in a metal carryall kept near the shower. This is a bath-cum-dressing room for a couple who have different morning schedules. "He likes to make early morning phone calls so we put a phone, as well as a built-in radio, in the wall next to the bench," says Halperin. Near the bath, Halperin had a sleek mahogany bureau built to fit against the wall (left) and above it she concealed clothing storage behind mirrored doors.

bottles that deserve to be seen: The soft colors and curved shapes of rows of pretty containers on open shelves add an alluring design element. Utilitarian items such as cotton balls and swabs, emery boards, and lotion take on new glamour when they are transferred to glass or silver containers. But the apothecary-like assortment of prescriptions and potions that tends to accumulate in most homes is best concealed within a medicine chest or a cupboard—preferably one with a roomy, well-illuminated interior.

"I wanted this to be a room to luxuriate in—not just a place to brush your teeth," says Manhattan designer Vicente Wolf. Overcoming the room's fairly limited size, Wolf shoehorned in remarkable storage (opposite). A linen closet was carved out at one end of the room. Wolf maximized its capacity by running the interior shelf space up to the ceiling. The designer brought in a table of his own design (above) that ingeniously serves multiple organizing purposes. Its broad top is a counter for a bowl of potpourri, a vase of flowers, and a lamp—also of Wolf's own design. Beneath, two *étagère*-like shelves hold bath linens, toiletries, and reading material.

Because the bath is a room with fitted fixtures, it is worthwhile to plan storage carefully and imaginatively. A vanity cabinet under the sink offers a natural storage opportunity. Boston designer William Hodgins likes vanities that are high and wide; their roomy depths provide plenty of under-counter storage, including space for a built-in clothes hamper. In bathrooms with pedestal sinks, alternate storage systems must be devised. Designer Mario Buatta might move a corner cupboard into a bathroom or build cabinets high on the upper walls. Room for less conventional bathroom amenities should be considered: A radio or television needs a secure shelf. Music enthusiasts may want stereo speakers in the wall. And a telephone and intercom are conveniences for some, necessities for others. Planning generously goes far in making a bathroom comfortable and functional. The most pampering baths are inevitably those with a variety of organizing elements—a spacious vanity surface, numerous towel bars and shelves, plus a wealth of hooks, pegs, and drawers placed wherever one is likely to reach for a fresh washcloth, a bar of herbal soap, or a fluffy robe.

The mood may be ethereal in the blue-tiled bathroom of Milan architect and design consultant Paola Navone, but the storage is definitely down to earth. When she renovated her loft home, Navone inserted shelves into a niche above the bathtub to display her collection of Provençal faïence, which is tinted a variation of the serene Mediterranean blue that appears in every room of her home. Behind the semi-opaque doors of a white-painted cabinet, probably once intended for hospital use, folded towels and assorted jars and bottles are arranged. Parading on top of the cabinet is a line of apothecary jars with candylike Murano glass finials and a trio of large, quirky architectural spires.

The soigné stylishness of designer
Anthony Antine's master bathroom (left) is
heightened by a vanity chest Antine
bought "as is" from an antiques dealer.
The top had been severely damaged in a
fire, so it did not diminish the chest's value
to fit it with a vanity basin. Toiletry items
are concealed on shelves Antine had built
inside the chest. Then the chest was
transformed by decorative painter John
Certa, who designed the chinoiserie effect
and created the illusion of old lacquer that
has started to age and lift. The lacquered
top of the chest (above) is the perfect
lustrous surface for displaying a trove of
Victorian silver and tortoise shell boxes.

playful decorum

WHEN IT COMES TO CASUAL ELEGANCE, INTERIOR designer Carolyn Guttilla is a masterful performer, known for rooms that are comfortable, yet chic—places where you can put up your feet and relax. She likes to mix custom-built sofas and bolts of decorator silk with items from flea market stalls, antiques shops, and even the occasional thrift shop. "Second-hand treasures," says Guttilla, "take the sting out of decorating." Underscoring her discomfort with decorating that is too pat, Guttilla includes hand-workmanship in her rooms, even sometimes picking up the paint brush herself. The designer is a highly accomplished decorative painter.

Guttilla's skill is seen in the design and storage planning of the bathrooms in her own Locust Valley, New York, weekend house. "It was an opportunity to fulfill my fantasy," says Guttilla about the revival of her own 1909 under-the-eaves bath.

"In such a sweet charming space, I didn't want a traditional medicine cabinet," says Guttilla. Nor did she want a wooden vanity chest; she wanted something softer. Guttilla found the solution in several yards of khaki-colored silk taffeta, which she turned into a

As romantic as a ballgown, the rustling silk taffeta skirt encircling the sink in designer Carolyn Guttilla's bathroom hides shelves of storage baskets. Stacks of lingerie nestle inside the painted bureau. Guttilla designed the room as a decidedly feminine contrast to her husband's bath, which is a study in crisp, tailored blue and white.

lushly gathered skirt for the sink. Shelves under the skirt contain

baskets holding toiletries. An additional bathroom storage element

is provided by the lingerie bureau, an unassuming, hardworking

piece that Guttilla refined by brushing on a faux bois finish.

Yet another of Guttilla's transformations with paint is the small

bureau in her husband's bathroom. The newly painted finish makes

it look like a 19th-century antique. Having a chest for clothing

allows each bath to act as a separate dressing room. "You don't dis-

turb each other," says Guttilla, "and it is very nice to have your lin-

gerie there when you come out of the shower."

Inspired by the colors in the tile floor of her husband's bath, Carolyn Guttilla handpainted an old chest and dotted the front with spiffy white ceramic knobs (opposite). With four drawers, it is an ideal haberdashery chest to organize socks, sweat suits, swim trunks, and weekend wear. Occupying a place of honor in the bedroom, an old chest painted with roses (right) provides a note of romantic storage. "It's a 19th-century antique that someone painted in the 1920s," says Guttilla.

bedrooms

personal retreats

SENSUOUS, DREAMY, SOOTHING—TODAY'S IDEAL bedroom is a haven we repair to in order to refresh and renew ourselves. In the ever-larger houses rising in suburban and country landscapes, the master bedroom is an increasingly alluring retreat with bathrooms, dressing rooms, and walk-in closets. It has become an area so spacious that it often includes a separate sitting room for reading, watching television, letter writing, listening to music. And in a healthy trend, more and more often the master bedroom suite contains a home gymnasium with equipment for various workout sessions.

With so much happening in the bedroom, storage is a greater issue than ever before. Designers solve the multiple storage requirements of the modern bedroom with a well-calibrated combination of built-in storage—both concealed and open—and furniture. "I try to outfit any closet to maximize space as if it were an ocean liner where every inch is precious," says Manhattan designer DeBare Saunders. He often adds an armoire with a honeycomb of built-in slots and drawers sized to shelter not only a wardrobe but also a horde of indispensible modern

Long before there were closets, bedrooms were outfitted with majestic armoires and wardrobe cabinets to house clothing necessities. These freestanding pieces are still a fine solution for creating storage space. Anchoring the stretch between two windows in the city apartment of Lee Bailey, a tall English pine cabinet serves the role of a classic armoire. The large basket above the cabinet invites further hidden storage possibilities.

When the storage challenge is not a lack of closet space but the absence of the closet itself, invention takes over. Without closets in her 18th-century Channel Island getaway off the coast of France, designer Barbara Wirth added shelves and hanging space to the corner of a guest room (opposite) and concealed them with a curtain hung from a wooden valance. ● Designer Nancy Braithwaite reinvented the closet door (left) by installing a pull-up shade of woven grass for an opening too cramped to accommodate the swing of a wooden door. The space-saving design also ties the closet area to the rest of the master bedroom, whose windows are dressed with light-filtering shades of the same softly textured cloth.

electronic equipment—cassette player, stereo, television, and VCR.

Personal taste and lifestyle ultimately dictate the specific closets, cabinets, and storage furniture a bedroom needs. For those who like a snug haven in which to nestle, designer Mario Buatta creates a cocoon by anchoring a bed within a deep niche and building cupboards on either side of it, with fronts that can be wallpapered.

Although the sidelines are the most popular spots for bedtime storage, they are by no means the only ones. Preferring the convenience of head-of-bed storage, Boston designer Ken Kelleher fashioned open-display niches crowned by closed cabinets (opposite) in his studio apartment.

● Patricia Trainor placed a mahogany chest at the end of her brass and iron antique bed (right). The surface holds a bouquet and a stack of bedtime reading while the deep drawers hide a wardrobe of lingerie and accessories. The bureau also acts as a buffer, separating the sleeping area from the rest of the room.

Someone who is an avid reader will want at least a Canterbury for newspapers and magazines and a small bookcase—and maybe even built-in bookshelves. A designated home for exercise equipment makes workouts easier by saving the fitness buff precious time. And the creative spirit who awakens with brainstorms in the night will appreciate a space nearby with niches and drawers for note pads and pencils as well as a work area for a personal computer or laptop.

With carefully thought-out storage, a bedroom can be truly a private pied-à-terre, a place to revive the spirit for another day.

the art of cabinetry

A FINELY BUILT WARDROBE WALL NOT ONLY performs a storage function, it also introduces great character and beauty to a bedroom. Sculptural panelled doors, expertly book-matched veneers, and rich dentil trim are details of the cabinet-maker's artistry that lend a sumptuous look to the room. The wardrobe's interior is important too. Ideally, it should combine a high degree of finishing along with function. Upper and lower hanging rods; niches for shoes, handbags, and hats; pull-out baskets or cabinet drawers for accessories; racks for ties and belts; and shelves for sweaters, shirts, and extra bedding—all are essential. Designers plan closet space by measuring a client's individual pieces of clothing, allowing each item its width and depth, and then adding at least 10 percent for new purchases. "The tendency," says designer DeBare Saunders, "is not to deaccession. People always accumulate more." Finally, generous lighting within the various cabinets and closets, perhaps activated when the door is opened, will reveal all immediately.

To maximize storage in a New York City apartment, architects Lee Mindel and Peter Shelton designed a sweep of built-in cabinetry. They played cut-outs of drawers and doors against large sections of raised panel woodwork, creating pattern of superimposed rectangles. Piercing the cabinet wall is the glass door to the bathroom which, along with the clerestory-style windows visible above the wardrobe, provides the adjoining room with light.

The mood may be casual at the vacation house of designer Christian Liaigre, yet not an inch of storage space is wasted. Inspired by the location of the house—on the Île de Ré, a small island off the French Atlantic coast—Liaigre paid tribute to the resourceful design of seaside houses and seagoing vessels. In the upstairs bath (above) shared by three bedrooms, metal hooks are numbered so guests can readily identify their towels. A muscular teak vanity displays three deep, below-counter drawers for toiletries. In a guest room (opposite), an overhead gallery exhibits an assortment of baskets. Where to store a wooden oar? On two large wooden hooks fastened to a whitewashed panelled wall.

PHOTOGRAPHS IN SILVER FRAMES, trinkets gathered during summers in Europe, a baby's mug filled with fragrant garden roses—these are among the keepsakes that make a bedroom warm and personal. To keep mementos close and organize other necessary items—a clock, a lamp, a night carafe—well-conceived storage at bedside is indispensable.

Nightstands are hosts to so many of our most beloved possessions. Manhattan designer Mario Buatta flanks his romantically canopied and chintz-draped beds with bedside tables about 20 by 30 inches, featuring shelves underneath and a drawer that opens either to the front or to the side. "You can get a lot of storage in it," he says of the table, which he has custom-built. Boston designer William Hodgins uses several different styles of bedside table, but they all must share the same features. "It's absolutely important that it be as big as possible, that it have a drawer and a shelf below to hold a wastebasket," says Hodgins.

bedside comfort

A surround of bookcases transforms the bedroom of antiquarian G. R. Durenberger into a retreat devoted to reading and relaxation. The wall at one end of the room (opposite) has three bays of bookcases in addition to an upper shelf that turns the area near the cathedral ceiling into storage for oversized volumes. Behind the bed, there are built-in shelves (above), as well as a ledge for a reading lamp and more books.

With its ingenious design, a demi-lune bedside table fits snugly against the wall (opposite), yet its multiple shelves hold a large bedtime library. Designers Lee Bierly and Christopher Drake included enough surface to accommodate a full-size lamp and various personal items. ● From his upholstered sleigh bed (above), collector Roger Lussier can enjoy the bibelots displayed in a Danish cupboard—tiny porcelain furniture called "farings." The fresh, leafy green interior of the cupboard is a surprising stroke in Lussier's serene beige-and-cream toned room.

Often the designer attaches sturdy castors so that the table can be moved easily aside when the bed is being made.

Another appealing design is the demi-lune–shaped nightstand with several lower shelves that Boston designers Lee Bierly and Christopher Drake created. They frequently have it custom-made for their clients' bedrooms. "It's a pretty shape with soft rather than hard edges, which is nice to have next to a bed," says Bierly. To further expand storage potential, he and his partner also try to work into a bedroom a round table that may be up to four feet in diameter. "You can put a dozen photographs on it," says Bierly, "and the table can still be used as a work surface or to eat at." Add a lamp, a pleasant view, a comfortable chair, and a warm pot of tea, and the result is definitely a room of one's own.

two
options

flexible accommodation

Light walls and floors (opposite) are foils for the oversize furnishings and belongings of a big family like Walter Chatham's. To house their large library, Chatham created shelving, painting the back wall of the shelves a vibrant yellow that sets off books and objects handsomely (above). A small study is tucked behind the bookcases. Easy-to-reach open and closed storage in the kitchen (overleaf) makes a colorful display of the cookware.

THE SPIRITED WAY IN WHICH STORAGE can bring color and pattern into a room is apparent in the walls of open shelves that architect Walter Chatham designed in the renovation of his SoHo loft. He and his wife, artist and millinery designer Mary Adams Chatham, were pioneers in the Manhattan area south of Houston Street when they converted their first loft space in the early 1980s. As their three children grew older, the Chathams went loft-hunting again. This time, they found the enormous, untouched, raw space they wanted in the top floor of an abandoned power plant. "It was such a wreck," says Mary, "that no one had lived in it for ten years."

The architect revamped this derelict industrial shell into a home for his lively family by transforming it into three main areas—the parents' master suite; an open-plan kitchen, dining, and living area; and, near the loft's entrance, a children's area that incorporates bedrooms which are wrapped around a wide, 30-foot-long hall that serves as both a gym-like exercise area and playroom.

"Living with our children is teaching me to operate more intuitively," says the architect. "Color and light are the most joyful aspects of architecture." To wash the interior in light, Chatham added a wall of windows and four immense skylights, then blasted color on the open walls of storage. Throughout the loft, shelving units are both functional and decorative. For instance, the quirky collectibles Mary turns up in antiques shops share shelf space in the living area with the couple's large library. In the kitchen, glassware, dishes, and crockery rest on open shelves occupying an entire wall; in the master bedroom, the bright-green open shelves display Mary's passion—a lovingly assembled collection of hats and hat boxes.

Fulfilling Walter's joyful vision of architecture, all these colorful storage walls perform two functions: They keep the Chathams' many cherished possessions in order and they tie together the large open spaces, injecting into the former power plant the exuberance of a big active family in the artistic community of New York City.

The open shelves in the bedroom are a stylish background for Mary Adams Chatham's hats. Her vast collection is treated like art, and a part of it is always on view. Drawers organize accessories and lingerie. The harlequin-pattern cabinet is crafted of pine and veneered with Formica. Its doors conceal a mirror and drawers full of Mary's treasures.

the science of storage

BRUCE BIERMAN DESIGNED HIS OWN New York loft to embrace the clean, spare architecture he admires. Spare, however, does not mean spartan. Bierman won't do without the "necessities" of life—a Sub-Zero refrigerator/ freezer, a washer and dryer, and a walk-in closet and dressing room. He squeezed them all into the 1100-square-foot living area of the long, narrow loft space that's as deftly conceived, and elegantly outfitted, as a yacht. Consider the kitchen: It does not look like a kitchen at all. "I wanted it," says the designer, "to look like a buffet in a dining room." It does. The island floats on two large steel columns. A wall running parallel to the buffet counter appears to be a series of attractive vertical wood panels: A full kitchen dwells beneath. The panels conceal the refrigerator, washer, and dryer. Deep shelves hold dishes, food, and recycling receptacles. Up high, rectangular panels lift up like the overhead caddies in an airplane, inviting additional storage for less-frequently used kitchenware.

What appears to be wood-sheathed walls in designer Bruce Bierman's Manhattan loft is a bank of cabinets faced in golden textured African anegre wood (opposite). The doors open to reveal a full kitchen (above) that includes a dishwasher and other appliances plus an array of built-in spaces for cooking equipment. Black granite covers the surface of the long serving island.

In the combination dressing room and walk-in closet, Bierman fitted the sliver of space with rods, shelves, and hooks in a way that utilizes every inch of storage potential. Rows of shelves present sweaters, shirts, and other folded clothing. Drawers in the vanity slide out to show off their contents, arranged by color, between smooth wood dividers. Mirrors and overhead lighting enhance the atmosphere. If a dressing room can be called svelte, Bierman's is. It could inspire the most careless dresser to reach for a new standard of sartorial organization.

Bruce Bierman planned the storage of his bathroom and adjoining walk-in closet to function as a well-organized dressing room. Adjustable glass shelves for sweaters make narrow closet bays appear airier and more spacious (opposite). The vanity's drawers (left) are thirty-six inches deep, a measurement Bierman frequently uses because it allows more storage than the typical twenty-four inch depth.

directory

OF DESIGNERS AND ARCHITECTS

DD Allen
New York, New York

Anthony Antine
Fort Lee, New Jersey

Christian Badin, Barbara Wirth
Paris, France

Linda Banks
Norwalk, Connecticut

Barbara Barry, Inc.
Los Angeles, California

Lou Ann Bauer
Bauer Interior Design
San Francisco, California

Beckhard Richlan & Associates
New York, New York

Charles Beresford-Clark, Inc.
London, England

Lee Bierly, Christopher Drake
Boston, Massachusetts

Bruce Bierman Design, Inc.
New York, New York

Laura Bohn
Lembo Bohn Design Associates
New York, New York

Agnes Bourne, Geoffrey DeSousa
San Francisco, California

Nancy Braithwaite Interiors
Atlanta, Georgia

Mario Buatta
New York, New York

Dan Carithers
Atlanta, Georgia

Walter Chatham
New York, New York

Fu-Tung Cheng
Berkeley, California

Maddalena De Padova
Milan, Italy

Joan DesCombes
Archictectural Artworks
Winter Park, Florida

Robert Dripps
Batesville, Virginia

Mary Douglas Drysdale
Drysdale Design Associates
Washington, D.C.

G.R. Durenberger
San Juan Capistrano, California

David Anthony Easton
New York, New York

William Ellis
New York, New York

Peter Ermacora, Evan G. Hughes
Norfolk, Connecticut

Heather Faulding
New York, New York

Tom Fleming
Irvine, Fleming and Jackson
New York, New York

Tricia Foley
New York, New York

Jonathan S. Foster
New York, New York

Carol Glasser
Houston, Texas

Richard Gluckman Architects
New York, New York

Mariette Himes Gomez
New York, New York

Carol Gramm Design
Garrison, New York

Russell Grove
New York, New York

Carolyn Guttilla
Locust Valley, New York

Joan Halperin
New York, New York

William Hodgins
Boston, Massachusetts

Ian Ingersoll
West Cornwall, Connecticut

Hugh Newell Jacobsen
Washington, D.C.

Lynn Jacobson and Associates
New York, New York

Scott K. James
New York, New York

Ken Kelleher
Boston, Massachusetts

Kuth, Ranieri
San Francisco, California

Richard Keith Langham
New York, New York

Susan Lanier,
   Paul Lubowicki
El Segundo, California

Letelier-Rock Design, Inc.
New York, New York

Christian Liaigre
Liaigre Design Co.
Paris, France

Arrel Linderman
Boston, Massachusetts

Roger Lussier, Inc.
Boston, Massachusetts

Gretchen Mann Designs
Lyme, Connecticut

Paul Mathieu
Aix en Provence, France

Charles Morris Mount
Silver & Ziskind Architects
New York, New York

Paola Navone
Milan, Italy

Benjamin Noriega-Ortiz
New York, New York

Thomas O'Brien
Aero Ltd.
New York, New York

Charlotte Perriand
Paris, France

Katie Ridder, Peter Pennoyer
Katie Ridder Home Furnishings
New York, New York

Eve Robinson Associates Inc.
New York, New York

Safdie Rabines Architects
San Diego, California

John F. Saladino Inc.
New York, New York

De Bare Saunders
Stingray Hornsby Antiques
Watertown, Connnecticut

Monique and Sergio Savarese
Dialogica
New York, New York

Sudie Schenck
Boston, Massachusetts

April Sheldon Design
San Francisco, California

Peter Shelton, Lee Mindel
Shelton, Mindel & Associates
New York, New York

José Solis Betancourt
Washington, D.C.

Charles Spada Interiors
Boston, Massachusetts

Sarah Spongberg Interior Design
S. Dartmouth, Massachusetts

John Stedila, Tim Button
Stedila Design
New York, New York

Turnbull, Griffin, Haesloop
San Francisco, California

Yves-Germain Taralon
   Decoration
Richebourg, France

Patricia Trainor
Bellport, New York

T.F. Vanderbeck Antiques
   & Interiors
Hadlyme, Connecticut

Anne Marie Vingo
San Francisco, California

Peter Wheeler
P.J. Wheeler Associates
Boston, Massachusetts

Bunny Williams
New York, New York

Vicente Wolf Associates
New York, New York

photography

CREDITS

1	Antoine Bootz	77	John Hall	137-141	Langdon Clay
2	Mark Darley	78	Oberto Gili	142-144	Scott Frances
5	Judith Watts	79	Jacques Dirand	146-147	Fernando Bengoechea
6	Oberto Gili	80	Dominique Vorillon	148-149	Jeff McNamara
8	Bob Hiemstra	81	Thibault Jeanson	150-151	Oberto Gili
10-11	Antoine Bootz	82	Kari Haavisto	152-153	Tom McWilliam
12	Scott Frances	83	Fran Brennan	154-157	Lizzie Himmel
14	Jacques Dirand	84-85	Walter Smalling	158	Antoine Bootz
16	Feliciano	86	Antoine Bootz	160	Feliciano
18	David Livingston	87	Langdon Clay	162	Langdon Clay
19	J.D. Peterson	88	William Waldron	163	Michael Dunne
20	Jeremy Samuelson	89	Richard Felber	164	Antoine Bootz
22-23	Alexandre Bailhache	90	Antoine Bootz	165	Melanie Acevedo
24-28	Peter Margonelli	91	Michael Dunne	166	Langdon Clay
30-33	Scott Frances	92-93	Michel Arnaud	168-169	Jacques Dirand
34	Thibault Jeanson	94-95	Antoine Bootz	170-171	John Vaughan
35	Vicente Wolf	96	D. Duncan/	172	Eric Roth
36	Peter Margonelli		David Livingston	173	Thibault Jeanson
37-39	Robert Lautman	98	Jacque Dirand	174-180	Scott Frances
40-43	Michael Dunne	100	Thibault Jeanson	182-185	Andrew Bordwin
44-50	Antoine Bootz	101	Jeff McNamara	188	Peter Margonelli
52-55	Jon Jensen	102-104	Jon Jensen	191	Kari Haavisto
56	Alex Hemer	105	Tom McWilliam	192	Laura Resen
58-59	Peter Margonelli	106-107	Dominique Vorillon	Endpapers	Robert Lautman
60-61	Gordon Beall	108-111	Jeremy Samuelson		
62-63	Kari Haavisto	112	Peter Margonelli		
64	Walter Smalling	113	Alan Weintraub		
65	Thibault Jeanson	114-117	Tom McWilliam		
66	Victoria Pearson	118-119	Richard Felber		
67	Melanie Acevedo	120-123	Dale Berman		
68	Antoine Bootz	124-127	Paul Whicheloe		
69	Laura Resen	128	Tom McWilliam		
70-72	Peter Margonelli	130	John Vaughan		
74	Jeff McNamara	132-133	Oberto Gili		
75	Thibault Jeanson	134	Gordon Beall		
76	Watts/Estersohn	135-136	Antoine Bootz		

ACKNOWLEDGMENTS

House Beautiful would like to thank homeowners Kate Edelman Johnson, Joel Franklin and Ellen Fondiler, Susan Stringfellow, Jacques and Laurence Hintzy, Debra Niemann and David Brodwin, Lynne and David Madison, Pamela Robinson Specktor, Rita Halbright and Jonathan Och, Edith and Arthur Hooper, and Barbara and Jim Grodin.

Room on page 1 designed by Katie Ridder and Peter Pennoyer; page 2, Byron Kuth and Elizabeth Ranieri; page 5, Peter Wheeler; page 6, William Hodgins; page 8, Richard Gluckman; page 10, Carol Gramm; page 11, Maddalena De Padova; page 12, Russell Grove; page 188, Gretchen Mann; page 191, Tom and Pam Kline; page 192, Thomas O'Brien.

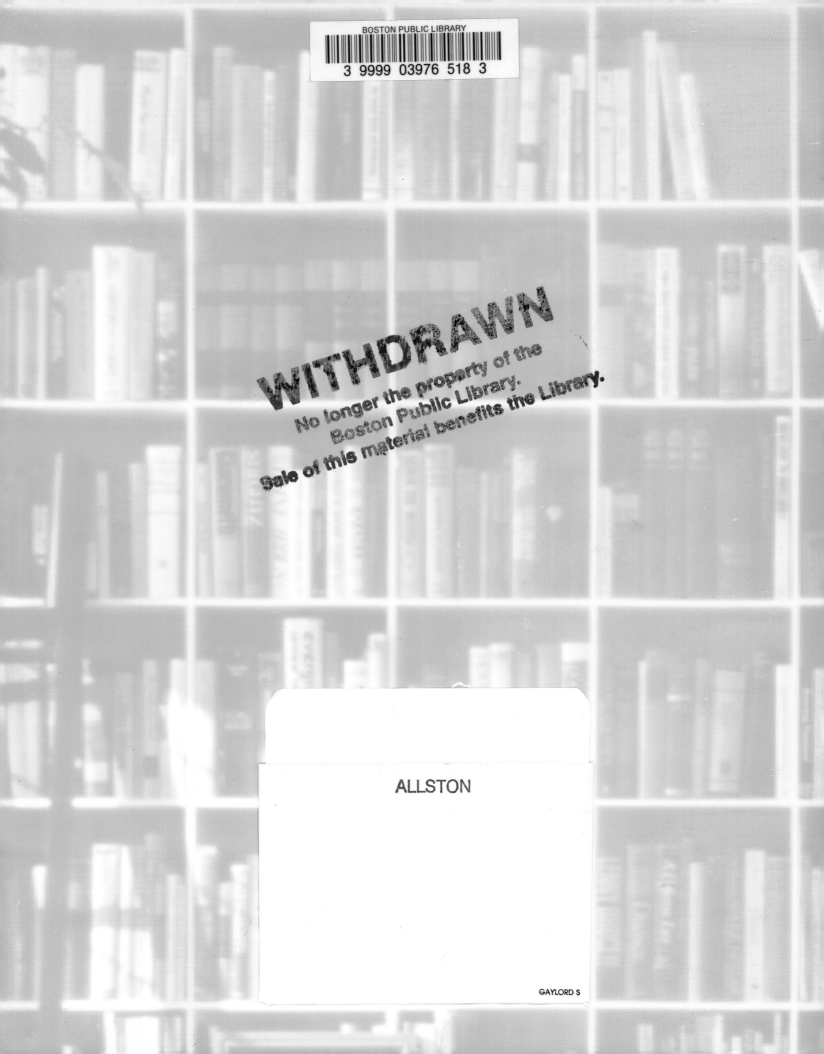